We Need Doctors

by Lola M. Schaefer

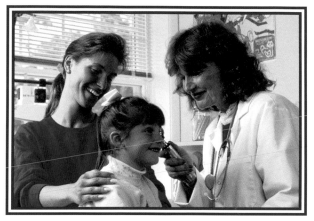

Consulting Editor: Gail Saunders-Smith, Ph.D.

Consultant: R. S. Lyle Hillman, M.D.
Diagnostic Radiologist
American Medical Association
Fellow, American College of Radiology

Pebble Books

an imprint of Capstone Press
Mankato, Minnesota

Pebble Books are published by Capstone Press
151 Good Counsel Drive, P.O. Box 669, Mankato, Minnesota 56002
http://www.capstone-press.com

2 3 4 5 6 07 06 05 04 03 02

Library of Congress Cataloging-in-Publication Data
Schaefer, Lola M., 1950–
    We need doctors/by Lola M. Schaefer.
    p. cm.—(Helpers in our community)
    Includes bibliographical references and index.
    Summary: Simple text and photographs present doctors and their role in
the community.
    ISBN 0-7368-0389-0
    1. Physicians—Juvenile Literature. 2. Medicine—Juvenile Literature.
[1. Physicians 2. Occupations.] I. Title. II. Series: Schaefer, Lola M., 1950– Helpers in
our community.
R690.S29 2000
610.69'52—DC21   99-19423
                                                                               CIP

Note to Parents and Teachers

The Helpers in Our Community series supports national social
studies standards for units related to community helpers and
their roles. This book describes and illustrates doctors and how
they help people. The photographs support early readers in
understanding the text. The repetition of words and phrases
helps early readers learn new words. This book also introduces
early readers to subject-specific vocabulary words, which are
defined in the Words to Know section. Early readers may need
assistance to read some words and to use the Table of Contents,
Words to Know, Read More, Internet Sites, and Index/Word List
sections of the book.

Table of Contents

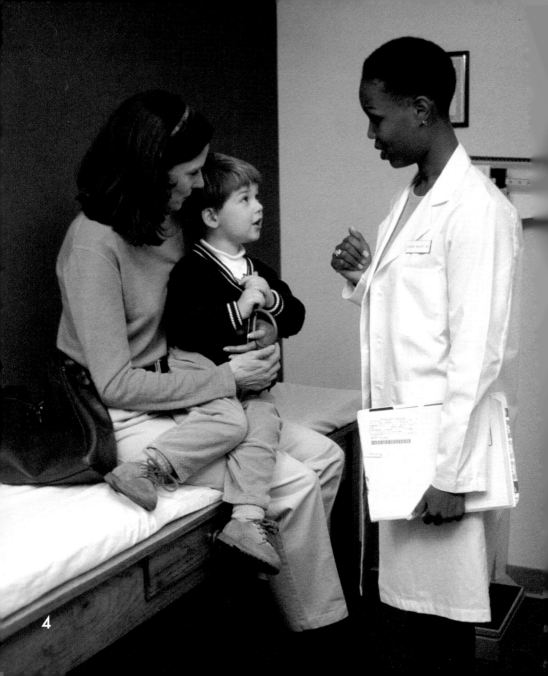

4

Doctors help people stay healthy.

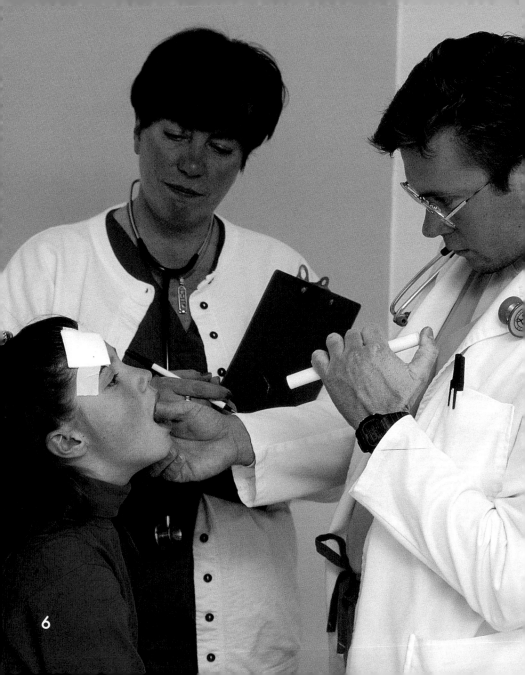

Doctors treat people
who are sick or hurt.

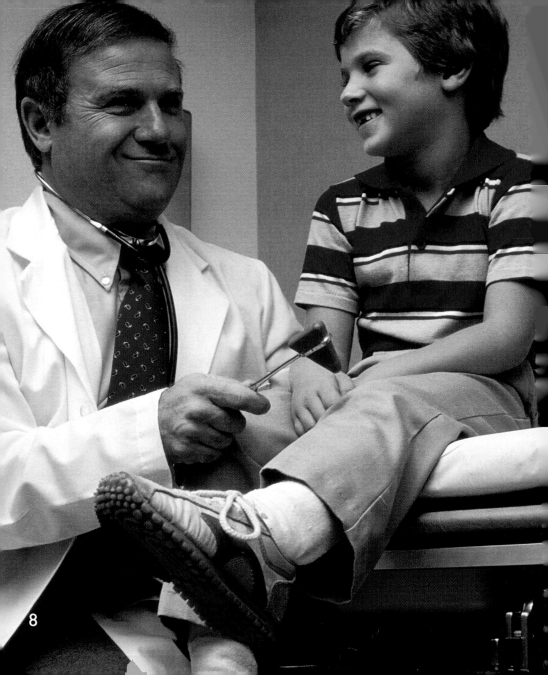

Doctors give checkups.

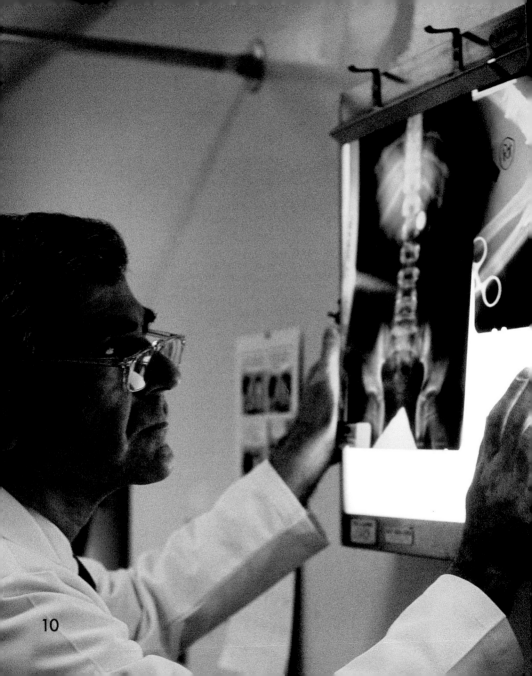

10

Doctors look at x-rays.

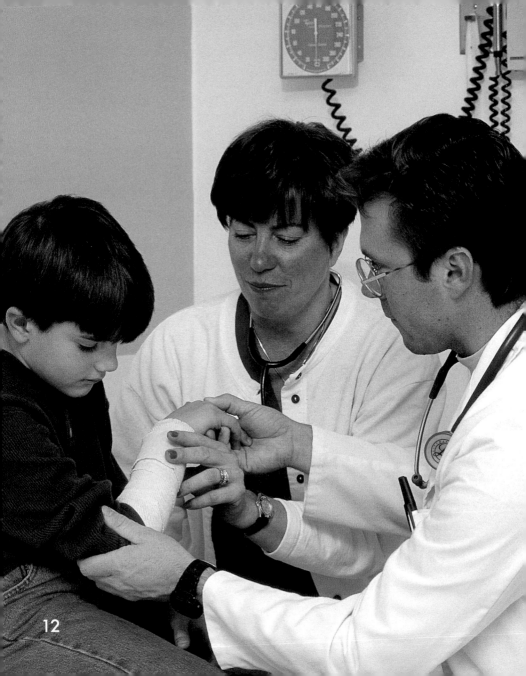

Doctors set broken bones.

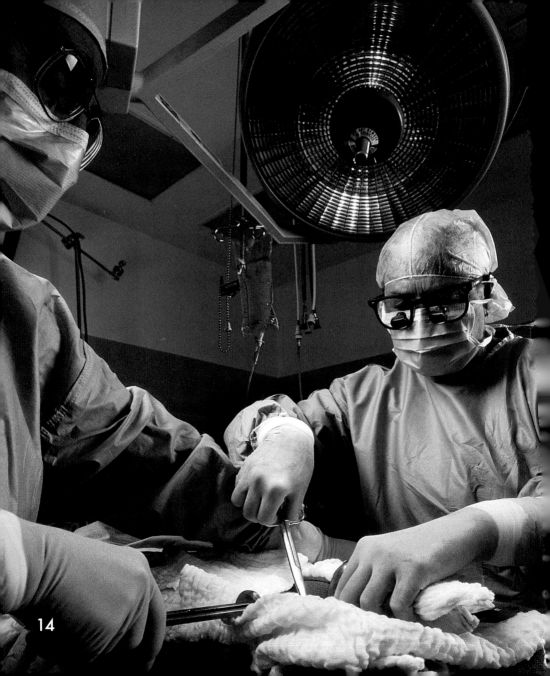

Doctors perform surgery.

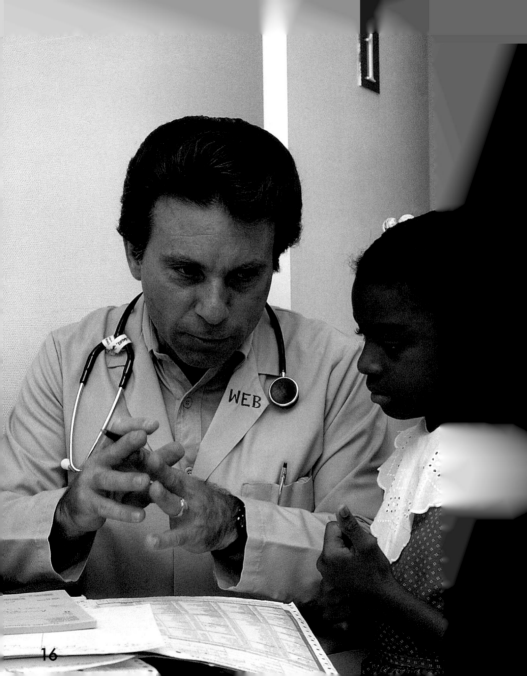

Doctors prescribe medicine.

Some doctors see patients in clinics.

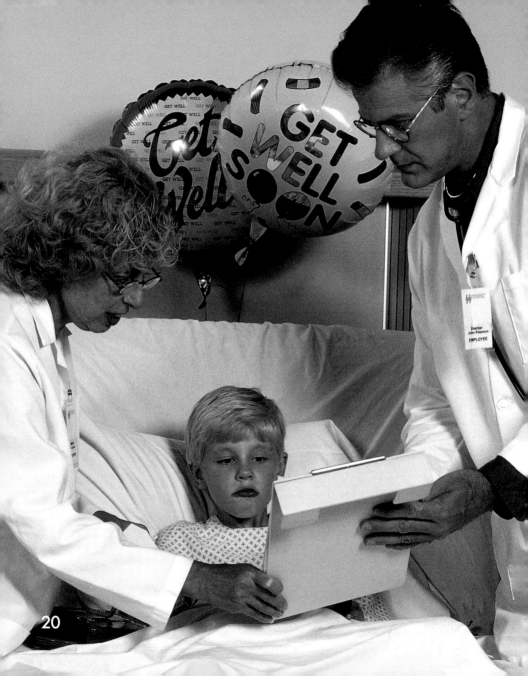

Some doctors see patients in hospitals.

Words to Know

clinic—a building where people go to receive medical care; some doctors have offices in clinics.

hospital—a place where people who are hurt or sick go; some doctors see patients in hospitals.

medicine—a drug that helps sick people get better

patient—a person who receives medical care

perform—to do something

prescribe—to order a medicine; doctors prescribe medicine for patients in their care; patients buy medicine at stores.

surgery—repairing or removing body parts that are sick or hurt

x-ray—a picture of the inside of a person's body; doctors use x-rays to see if bones are hurt or broken.

Read More

James, Robert. *Doctors.* People Who Care for Our Health. Vero Beach, Fla.: Rourke, 1995.

Moses, Amy. *Doctors Help People.* Plymouth, Minn.: Child's World, 1997.

Ready, Dee. *Doctors.* Community Helpers. Mankato, Minn.: Bridgestone Books, 1997.

Saunders-Smith, Gail. *The Doctor's Office.* Field Trips. Mankato, Minn.: Pebble Books, 1998.

Internet Sites

BLS Career Information: Doctor
http://stats.bls.gov/k12/html/sci_003.htm

KidsHealth—For Kids
http://kidshealth.org/kid/index.html

Your Gross and Cool Body
http://yucky.kids.discovery.com/noflash/body/index.html

Index/Word List

bones, 13
broken, 13
checkups, 9
clinics, 19
doctors, 5, 7, 9, 11,
   13, 15, 17, 19, 21
healthy, 5
help, 5
hospitals, 21
hurt, 7
medicine, 17

patients, 19, 21
people, 5, 7
perform, 15
prescribe, 17
see, 19, 21
set, 13
sick, 7
stay, 5,
surgery, 15
treat, 7
x-rays, 11

Word Count: 42
Early-Intervention Level: 9

Editorial Credits
Karen L. Daas, editor; Abby Bradford, Bradfordesign, Inc., cover designer;
   Kimberly Danger, photo researcher

Photo Credits
Comstock, Inc., cover
Index Stock Imagery, 6, 12, 18; Index Stock Imagery/Willie L. Hill, 16
International Stock/Greg Voight, 14
Jeff Kaufman/FPG International LLC, 1
Photo Network/Tom McCarthy, 8
Ron Chapple/FPG International LLC, 4
Unicorn Stock Photos/Tom McCarthy, 10, 20